BEFORE I BECAME ME

BEFORE I BECAME ME

The Path to My Greatness

Samuel E. Underwood

ARPress
ILLUMINATING IDEAS
EMPOWERING VOICES

ARPress
45 Dan Road Suite 5
Canton MA 02021
Hotline: 1(888) 821-0229
Fax: 1(508) 545-7580

Ordering Information:
Quantity sales. Special discounts are available on quantity purchases by corporations, associations, and others. For details, contact the publisher at the address above.

Printed in the United States of America.

ISBN-13:	Softcover	979-8-89330-000-0
	eBook	979-8-89330-002-4
	Hardcover	979-8-89330-001-7

Library of Congress Control Number: 2024900492

ACKNOWLEDGMENT

I would like to thank God for allowing me the strength and wisdom to write this book to help fellow substance abusers. I feel so proud to be able to use my past experiences to help others in their journey to meeting the right people that will become a part of their support system. I want to thank my wife, Kim Underwood, for her support. I also would like to thank all the people that helped me to my greatness the people that worked in the shelters, DayTop Village, and the courts and jails systems in New York City. I know they were just doing their jobs, but I appreciate them for the jobs they do. Without them taking those jobs, society would be a lot worse than it is now, so thank you again. Because of the times I went through those systems, I gained strength to become the man I'm today. Through those experiences, I'm writing this book to help others. I want to say a special thank-you to Margaret (Momma) Jackson—may she RIP. She became the mother I needed when my mother passed away.

The first time I experienced getting high was when I was about ten years old. I wasn't old enough to buy alcohol or knew someone who would give me drugs. I found some cigars and matches. You might say, what does that have to do with getting high? I would light the cigar and puff it really fast a couple of times. After the fourth puff, my head would start spinning around. At that time in my life, that was fun—a new experience that I liked. I liked it so much, I tried to do it every day if I could. Now as I look back at my life, I would say that was about the time I started on the wrong path in life.

Well, about a year before I started playing hooky from school (not attending school), I realized that I liked the feeling of control I felt when I didn't go to school. So if you really look into my life, the first time I got high was when I didn't go to school because after that, the smoking, girls, lying, robbing, stealing, and the drugs started. And it kind of started just like that—I stayed on that path for about twenty-three years. And it was exciting at times, but it was also dangerous. I can remember times I almost lost my life. So I'm grateful for being alive with most of the sense that God gave me. I didn't have to be that blessed; I could have been one of the unlucky ones that left this earth too early, but I was one of the ones selected to tell my story, so someone could maybe learn from some of the things I went through.

Like I stated before, I liked to play hooky. I was introduced to it when I was in the fourth grade.

A guy came up to me and asked me did I want to play hooky. I told him I didn't know what playing hooky was. He said with excitement in his voice, "You don't know what hooky is—then I'll be the first to show you." He showed me how to play, and I was hooked. I continued to play hooky throughout my time in school.

I was in the tenth grade; I was cutting class like I did every day. When a friend of mine started a fire in the boys' bathroom, he threw a match into the trash can. Now you know in those cans, it's mostly brown paper towels that will catch fire very quickly. Once I saw the flames from the fire, I told my friends, "You guys are bugging today. I'm going to class."

But there was a school aide in the hallway when we came out of the bathroom. He went into the bathroom after us; he put the fire out. I knew we were in big trouble because he knew my friend's name and mine. We were known as troublemakers in the school. He told the dean what we had done. He suspended us for five days. When they told me they were suspended, I told them that they should go to class like me. They said that the dean told them to tell me that I was suspended too. I said, "That's not fair because I was in class. I didn't start a fire. So why was I being punished?" I didn't complain anymore because I was in the bathroom when it happened.

So I accepted my punishment—it was only five days. I could do that with no problem. The problem wasn't the days out of school—it was how I would explain it to my mother. She was one of those mothers that didn't take any mess. She was a hardworking woman. She wanted her kids to be better than she was. I had to come up with a real good story or just tell the truth, so I told a little bit of both. I said that James, Charles, and I were in the bathroom, smoking a cigarette. When the school aide walked into the bathroom, he saw the trash can on fire, but he didn't see me throw the match in the trash can.

My mother looked at me and said, "You're full of shit, boy."

I said, "But, Mom, I'm telling the truth. I didn't start the fire in the bathroom."

She said, "Samuel, what do we do now?" I knew when she called me Samuel, I was in big trouble.

"We have to go to the school on May fifteenth at 9:15 a.m."

"Okay, that's fine—we can definitely make that appointment because I have some questions about your last report card."

I felt a little relieved—she didn't get upset. She didn't yell and scream—she just calmly said, "You're grounded until we go to your school and hear the other side of the story."

I was relieved for now, but I knew on May fifteenth, it would be a different story. So for that five-day period, I helped around the house. My mother even said, "You must be in some real big trouble at that school because you're like a different kid. You're helping around the house without me asking you. You're not harassing your sisters. The house is so quiet now. I wish it was like this all the time—not just when you're in trouble—but I love you, my son, for who you are."

The five days went by pretty fast. On May fifteenth, I woke up early. I'm not going to lie—I was nervous about going back to school. My mother was up cooking breakfast. I thought to myself, *This is my last meal before I die*, because I knew the meeting at the school would reveal a lot of the things I was doing at the school like cutting classes, smoking in the hallways—everything but going to class.

On our way to the school, we didn't talk much—just me giving her directions as we walked to the school. As we walked to the school, I saw some friends of mine. They started calling me Sam the Man and saying I was in big trouble. "You had to bring your mother to school." My mother gave me a look, and if looks could kill, I would have died that day. I just put my head down and continued to walk to my execution.

We finally reached the room we were told to go to. The room was filled with my teachers, school aide, guidance counselors, and every staff member that wanted to add their two cents to my death sentence. I was pissed off that all these people would want to tell on me. The dean asked my mother and me to sit down. He started by telling my mother that I have been absent 100 days from school and there were only 180 days in a school year. She looked at me and said, "I send him to school every morning—I don't know what happens."

I said, "I do go to school, but my homeroom class is at seven forty-five in the morning. If you missed that class, then you're absent for the whole day even if you go to all your other classes."

Then my English and Social Studies teachers jumped up to say, "He didn't come to my class either." My math and science teachers both nodded their heads in agreement. My gym teacher just shook his head, he said, "I told you this would happen." The straw that broke the camel's back was George. He was a part of a special program called The Spark Program where students could play ping pong or cards. It was a place you could kind of relax during the school day. I thought George was cool until he started telling my mother about some of the things he caught me and my friends doing. Like the time he caught us on the back staircase smoking weed. The reason we didn't get in trouble was because he just smelled the weed. He didn't actually see us smoking the weed.

To be totally honest, George was a real nice guy. He had been through some problems in his life. So he kind of understood us. That's why I feel we never got in trouble for that incident. George said he knew a place that would be a good fit for me, but let everyone speak to you first. The teachers and aides in the room started to tell their stories about me—how when I did come to class, I was moody, not really there. If I was asked to participate, I would get mad and leave the classroom. However, there were days I would be happy and ready to participate without being asked to. The aides also told of some of their experiences of dealings with me—how I'm always in the hallways, cutting class or doing something that I'm not supposed to be doing. Now that's when the trouble started with me because I'm asked to leave the place that I'm at. I would get upset, saying things like, "You guys are always bothering me. Why don't you go and harass someone else? Just leave me alone—I'm not bothering anyone."

"We tell him we are doing our job by keeping the hallways and other areas safe by making sure that no one is using these areas without permission. So if you feel like we're harassing you, please forgive us— we're just doing our job. He would then leave the place he was at, but he would always have the last word."

My mother looked at me then looked around the room. I could see she was starting to cry. She said, "I send him to school every morning. I try to give him a good life, teach him to want more out of life. I don't know where I went wrong. I just don't know what to do now."

That's when George said, "Mrs. Underwood, Sam is a good kid. I think you're doing a great job, but it's the people he's hanging around. They're a bad influence on him. I know a place that helped me through all of my problems. It's called DayTop Village, a drug treatment program. I know he's only smoking marijuana and drinking beers. That's how it starts, then they go to the stronger drugs like cocaine and heroin. It's a nice place in Upstate New York. The town is called Millbrook in Poughkeepsie, New York. He will be living in a mansion that was donated to DayTop to help people with drug problems."

She said, "That sounds like a good place for him to get help."

I said I didn't want to go—it would make me worse.

She looked at me and said, "You're going."

George said he would take care of everything. She could just go home and relax. Yea right—if she went home and relaxed, I would be very surprised. I just knew when I got home. I would get the ass whipping of my life. I'm not going to lie and say I wasn't nervous. I was very nervous. I was planning my strategy on how I would handle the ironing cord or the broom stick. Whichever one she decided to use, I was ready, thinking I would strip down to my underwear then lie across the bed and take my punishment like a man. I always thought like this: *Don't do the crime if you can't do the time.* So I was ready, but to my surprise when we got home, she told me to go to my room because she was tired of looking at me. I was happy that she didn't just start beating me like she did so many other times when I made bad choices. I was still nervous because I didn't know what was going to happen. She came into my room about two hours after. She had been crying. She told me that she loved me and she wanted the best for me. She was sending me to DayTop Village.

So I could have a chance at a better life. After I thought about it, I felt she was right. I did need a chance at a better life because the path I was following was rough sometimes. So we hugged each other and said we'd loved one another. She then went to her room—I didn't talk to her that much after that day. I think she felt like she hadn't been a good mother—I know she was a great mother. She gave me a strong foundation of values and principles. I was the one making the wrong choices. It wasn't her fault—she always told me the right path to follow. I was just hardheaded. Now look at where I'm going—DayTop Village. Damn, I fucked up! Packed and ready to go, we called a cab to take me to my destination. During the cab ride, we started to talk about our future and how everything would be different when I completed the program. I would come back home and start all over again with a new mindset. I just agreed with her because I was just thinking about what I was going to go through for the next two and a half years. Oh, I forgot to mention, yes, I'll be gone for two and a half years. That's a long time, and you can make a lot of changes in your lifestyle if you wanted to—and yes, I wanted to make changes ASAP. The cab rode up to the main entrance of DayTop Village. I was ready for whatever this place had to give.

We walked into the building. It was very elegant inside the lobby; there were mirrors on the walls and chandeliers in the high ceilings. I mean real old school design. We walked pass the swirled staircase to an office in the back of the building. We were told what I had to do, what the program would help me work on. My mother asked me was I ready for my new journey. I said yes, and she signed the papers to enroll me into the program. After she signed the papers we hugged, I told her I loved her, and she said she loved me too. We kissed, then she walked out of the office. Mr. Robinson started telling me that I would stay the night there. I would be leaving to go upstate around 3 p.m. tomorrow afternoon. I thought to myself, *I'm only fifteen years old.* This is a lot to deal with in such a short time, but I agreed to do it. So I have to stay focus on the path until I finished this program. I thought to myself, *Get a good night sleep to be ready in the morning.*

That morning, they woke me up at 6 a.m. I asked them why we woke up so early; they told me that successful people get up early to take advantage of most of the twenty-four hours in a day, so by 8am I had washed up and eaten breakfast. After eating breakfast, I lay down on the bed I slept in that night. This was new for me—getting up early wasn't my thing. That's one reason I was absent one hundred days from school, because my homeroom was at 7:45 a.m. in the morning and I always missed it. While I was lying there, I was checking out my surroundings. There were a lot of people in this building. They were like ants—everyone was moving with a purpose. The ones that passed by the room I was in all said, "Good morning and have a great day." I really got nervous was that going to be me in two and a half years? I thought that being nice to others wouldn't be that bad.

Then Mr. Robinson said, "Your journey is about to start. First, you're going to orientation to learn more about DayTop." It was from eight to twelve noon, and then I went to lunch. I met some people while I was eating lunch. They were telling me about the house I was going to live in for the next twelve to eighteen months. It was all up to me on how I behaved on a daily basis. They told me I looked like I would do fine. "Just stay focused on why you came to DTV and everything will be all right."

It was 2:45 p.m. I heard my name being called. "Samuel Underwood, your bus to Millbrook House is leaving in fifteen minutes." I was packed and ready to go. I was ready yesterday when my mother brought me here. I've been waiting on them, so don't start hurrying me now. That was just how I was thinking at that time in my life. I got on the bus and found me a window seat, so I could see all the things around me. It was a three-hour ride, but it took five hours. We had to make a couple of stops to pick up some other people. We stopped in Queens and in Staten Island. I thought I could stay up the whole ride, but I fell asleep.

When I woke up, they were telling me we're there. I got out of the bus. As I walked to the house I notice we were in the country. Nothing but trees, flowers, and dirt roads—totally different from the projects I lived in. I thought to myself, *This would be like summer camp*. Once I entered the house—oh, I forgot to tell you it was a very beautiful mansion. In the vestibule, a young man came up to me. He said to come with him. So I went with him to a room with a chair in the middle of it. He took my bags and he told me to sit down.

The room had one light that set behind the chair I was sitting in. There were five people sitting in the chairs in front of me on the other side of the room. I heard a female's voice asking me, "Why should you become a part of this house, our house?"

I said, "Because my mother signed the papers for me to come here."

She said, "Hell, no. It's not that easy for you to come into this house and take our love."

The other four voices said, "Yea, that's right."

I said to them, "I don't want your love. I'm here because my mother signed some papers."

The female's voice (who I later found out was Anna, a young Hispanic woman from the Bronx) said, "Tell us your story."

I said, "What you mean my story?"

Another voice said, "Why are you here sitting in front of us? And not because your mother signed some damn papers."

I said I was in the boy's bathroom in school, and a friend of mine (Charles) started a fire in the trash can.

"Charles, James, and I all got suspended from school, but I didn't start that fire."

He said, "You didn't start it, but you were there. Let me ask you something, Sam—you don't mind if I call you Sam, right."

I said it was all right.

"Okay, Sam, did you try to stop him from starting the fire, or you just watched him do it?"

"I just watched him do it."

"Why didn't you stop him? You didn't care about the school or the people in it. You're a selfish piece of shit. The whole school could have burned down and all you have to say is I didn't start the fire. Yes, yes, you would have still gone to jail for being a part of the incident—a conspirator—to the crime. That's what you were and you didn't even care."

The purpose of me going into that room was to break me down. so I could start feeling my emotions. They broke me down. When I left that room, I was feeling free. like a load had been lifted off of me. I mean they went deep into my life. I was only fifteen years old, but we talked about some things that made me cry. I thought to myself, *If this is how it's going to be here, then it won't be that bad because I'll be getting the cleaning that my soul needed.*

Now I was officially welcomed into the house. As I walked to my room, people in the house were saying, "Welcome to Millbrook." As I was walking, I saw people wearing signs and some of them were wearing costumes. I saw one guy with a costume that said he was a super sneak. He also had a sign around his neck describing what he had done. This was a totally new world for me. I stayed there for about a year. I learned a lot of things about myself, like I have a good nature toward other people. I realized that could be bad in the world of drugs and crime. People will take advantage of you; I would always feel like someone would be taking advantage of me. So I really never let anyone get close to me.

One thing I did when I was at DTV: I became an expeditor. This was one of the jobs in the house. I was the police (the eyes and ears) of the house. I would maintain the order of the house. If I saw something or someone doing something wrong, I would handle it. As an expeditor, I could give verbal lessons to the other people in the house. That position helped me grow as a person—it gave me more confidence. It also taught me to look at the situations before I reacted to a problem. DTV taught me values and principles—that's something I use every day of my life now. For the time I stayed there. I felt my mother made a good choice. It made me a better person overall.

Now I was being transferred to Manhattan House on Forty-First Street. I was excited about going back to New York City, but I was in another phase of the program. I had just completed phase one. Now I was going to phase two of the program. In phase two. I was back in NYC living on Forty-First Street where I started a year ago. I was slowly getting back into society by finding a job and going out on a daily basis.

To get back into the flow of the Big Apple, I also had some house duties like helping in the kitchen three times a week at dinnertime. The one thing I liked most was I could put in for a weekend pass. That's when everything ended at DTV—I was on pass with my mother. We went to some of her friend's house in Staten Island, New York. They were drinking and smoking weed. My mom wasn't smoking weed, but she was drinking. She got pretty wasted that day—she eventually fell asleep. I stayed with her to make sure she would be all right. She was my mother, and sons protect their mothers.

When I got back from my weekend pass, I was asked how my weekend went. I told them the truth. They got very upset with me, telling me I should have left and came back to the house. I told them I was with my mother, and I couldn't just leave her there. They told me for not leaving her in Staten Island and coming back to the house, I would be restricted to the house for one month. I would also have to wash pots every night after the dinner meal. I was pissed off because I felt they didn't look at it through my eyes. If that was their mother, would they have left her there? I felt they would have stayed like I did. I didn't want to, but I went along with the restrictions to my privileges.

Until I just got fed up with the bullshit at DTV, I had felt this feeling a lot of times when I was in the Millbrook House. But I couldn't leave—I was two and a half hours away from New York City. So I had to deal with those feelings back then now I was in the city. And my father worked nine blocks away from the Manhattan House. Now that was one of the things I should have worked on when I was upstate: how I could convince myself to do things that weren't good for me, like leaving the program to go home. Like I said it wasn't a good idea, now that I look back on my life. I was my worst enemy, always getting myself in trouble. I learned how to hide that person when I was upstate.

Being around more experienced street people, I learned some tricks of the street game. For example: if you're going to tell a lie, start putting it together a couple of days before you actually tell the lie. That way it appears like you're telling the truth. So days before I left DTV, I was making up all the bad reasons DTV wasn't good for me anymore. I was going to my father's job. He was always easier to convince than my mother. And everything he knew about DTV, I told him, so it would be easy to tell him some of the bad things about that place. Now that I think about it, I was also very good at splitting my parents. I realized that they didn't really talk to each other. I was always the middleman between them. So I learned how to make that work for me, and it worked fine. I would tell my father about things my mother did. Then there would be times I would have some juicy information about my father. One thing I did know was they still loved each other in a kind of a strange way.

On my way to his job, I was preparing myself. I would have to look him straight in his eyes. When I started telling the story, it was a lie, but it felt better if I called it a story. I got to my father's job. I told him the story, and he believed me. He gave me the keys to his apartment. As I was riding the train to the Bronx, I thought about how I was going to tell my mom why I left the program. She would be angry at me because she thought I was doing well in the program. And I was doing fine until the incident with her. I hoped she would understand the story when I explained it to her—how it was kind of her fault I left the program.

I didn't even tell my dad about what happened in Staten Island. I guess I was always thinking of my parent's feelings. I didn't want them to go through any more pain than they would have to. I have put them through enough. I thought to myself when I saw her, I would deal with that issue. I've been home for two weeks now. The first week was the worst; DTV was calling my mother's house almost every day, telling her that I just walked out of the program without permission to leave, and they should make me come back to finish the program. My parents came to me to ask me what I wanted to do; I said I didn't want to go back. I told them if they let me stay out, I would be good. I wouldn't cause any problems. I told them I was at DTV for a year, I learned a lot of things about drugs. How they can hurt you and why you should stay away from them. I told them they could trust me. I was ready to be a productive young man.

I lied to them because as soon as I saw my old friends, I was back to my old tricks, getting high and soon after I was getting into trouble. That's what always happens to me. The first time I got high again, I didn't take a lot. My system was clean. I hadn't gotten high in a year. So just a little of beer and weed, and I was on cloud nine. I really regret I didn't complete DTV. Because it started: me always starting something, but never finishing them. That trait has followed me throughout my life. I look back to see many uncompleted things in my life. If I could take back one thing in my life, I would have completed DTV. I believe I would have never lived the life that I lived. Because I would've had a strong support system, a foundation that would help you fights your issues when you're weak and ready to give up. Now I'm back in the real world. I realized I didn't have it together like I thought I had. I started noticing that DTV was a controlled environment, and things were handled differently than on the street. I was finding it hard to cope with the everyday life on the streets. I wanted and needed to ask for help, but my pride came into play. I wouldn't let myself look like a failure—not me, Sam the Man. So I went back to what was comfortable and easy for me.

I started getting high every day—I mean I got so fucked up, so I didn't have to deal with the issues I experienced on a daily basis. Like a lack of confidence when it came to approaching a female—I would get so nervous. I would freeze up, not being able to move, but with beers like Old English 800. I could approach the ladies with no problems. The beer helped me work through a lot of my problems, but it was also the gateway to harder drugs. Because the beers didn't get me as high as I wanted to be anymore, so I started stiffing cocaine and heroin. I liked cocaine, but my favorite was heroin: P-Funk—that's what we called it. It made me feel warm and fuzzy all over my body. It was a great feeling. That later made me homeless, robbing and stealing. I also sold drugs. So yes, the drugs gave me that great feeling. It also gave me the confidence I needed on a daily basis. I look at the price I paid for that pleasure—damn, what a price to pay.

I forgot to mention how many times I overdosed on speedballs. Yes, I graduated to shooting drugs in my veins. Now this was the ultimate high you could get without dying. And I also did that a couple of times—almost died. I remember one time I woke up early because it was check day. Today I would pick up my welfare benefits. I would have some money in my pockets to do some things I wanted to do for myself, like getting a haircut and buying some personal items like soap and deodorant and maybe a pair of pants or a shirt. Damn, all that sounded good the day before I was going to do all those things. Until I got that damn money in my hands, I would start getting sick and needed the drugs to feel normal, and the drugs won again.

I jumped on the train to go to Fifty-Seventh Street and Eighth Avenue to pick up my check. Now that I had it, I copped a bag of P-Funk to get me normal. Now I needed some cocaine, so I bought a dime of coke. Now I needed an empty bottle, so I could put some water in it and also use the top to cook the coke in. I got everything I needed. Now I go into the projects to the roof. I needed a quiet and safe place I could get high in. I cooked up the coke and tied up. I hit my arm once or twice to wake up the veins. I stuck the needle in my arm. I felt the rush of the coke, it was such a good feeling. I liked to boot the coke to get that rush. It's like you get higher when you boot coke. All of a sudden, I started feeling lightheaded—now I was passing out. I started to stumble down the stairs. I hit my head on the wall, but I wouldn't sit down. I was by myself—if I sat down, I might not be here today. I finally made it out of the building. I was thankful that I didn't die in that stairway.

So I brought a beer and another bag of P-Funk to celebrate. Now isn't that kind of fucked up? I almost overdosed a few minutes ago and now I'm celebrating. Damn, that just shows how my addiction took over my life. I was a very sick person on a path to destroying myself. But do you know what was the worst? I thought I was cool. I was Sam the Man, but really, I was a scared little boy that was on a path to killing myself. And I didn't even know I was doing it—now that's real messed up if you want to be real.

To show you the path was real, I had another near-death experience. I was on Forty-Fourth Street and Eighth Avenue selling pills. I would go to the doctors, mostly psychiatrists, so I could get valiums that I could sell to other people. I was selling my pills one day when I saw this beautiful young lady. I walked up to her and said, "I'm Sam the Man."

She said her name was Toni. I asked her if she wanted to have a cup of coffee or something to eat. She said yes, and the romance started. It was more of a sex thing than anything else. I would get high off the P-Funk, and I would become Super Dick. I mean I could fuck for hours without stopping. And Toni loved it because she was a freak. I didn't mean that in a bad way. She was a good mother. She took care of her kids and sometimes other people's kids too. She was also the person who introduced me to Methadone. She would give me some of her weekend supply that would hold me for a couple of hours. I didn't have to get a bag of P-Funk to feel normal. At this period in my life, feeling normal was easy. I was using anything to keep that feeling. I used pills, beer, and alcohol, but heroin and cocaine were number one on my list.

I was hanging out with Toni. She gave me some of her weekend supply of methadone. She didn't know that, I had brought eighty milligrams of methadone of my own. So when she offered, I knew I should have said no, but I was an addict. I loved to get high. So when she offered, I couldn't say no. She didn't know I had been taking pills and spitting the eighty milligrams of meth I had brought. I had the pills—I had taken the meth that I had been spitting on. I also had drunk a quart of beer, the malt liquor kind. I was feeling good like I was on cloud nine. I was mellow, so I decided to lie down to really enjoy this feeling I was experiencing.

I don't remember much of what happened, but I remember being shot in my arm with a solution that woke me up quickly. The emergency medical technicians asked me a couple of questions, like what is your name and where was I at right now. I answered the questions correctly, so they didn't take me to the hospital. However, they told me I had overdosed on a mixture of pills, methadone, and alcohol. How they had to give me a shot to bring me back to life. They told me how lucky I was and to be careful with what I put in my body. I thanked them for their help, thinking to myself how I had just played chess with death and won this time.

Now I'm going back upstairs to Toni's room. I didn't tell you before—she lived in a Welfare hotel called the Prince George Hotel. So me having overdosed in her room wasn't a good thing at all. I knocked on the door. She told me that I couldn't stay with her anymore because I was going to get her and her three kids kicked out of the hotel. She said they would be on the streets because of my stupidity. I told her I was fine. She made me sit in the hallway for about an hour. Then she let me come back into her world again.

I would like you to look at my path of self-destruction. I was trying to kill myself, and I didn't even know it. I thought I was having fun getting high. I was putting a mother and her three kids' lives in danger of being put on the street (homeless). Now you know when you mess up your welfare case, it's hard for you to get things back in place, so you could understand why she didn't want me in her life. But I think she liked me a lot, or was it the way I made her feel when we had sex? However, she felt, it didn't matter to me at the time. I was doing what Sam the Man wanted to do, and that's all that mattered back then. I did care about others' feelings—I used the drugs to hide behind my feelings. In the streets, you can't show any feelings. You have to be hard as a rock like you don't care.

I did care—that's why I'm here to tell my story. I wasn't tough like I needed to be on the street. I just liked to get high. It was a time I was selling drugs on the corner. I was having a pretty good day. I had flipped three bundles of crack. My pockets were getting fat with money. Then this guy I knew named T came by to say hello. I knew him, but I didn't feel comfortable when he was around my stash (drugs) because we sold drugs for the same people. I went to serve a customer, and my stash was gone. I looked around—there was no one around to blame. I had thoughts, but no facts to support them. Now, what do I do—go to the man and tell him that someone stole my stash? That would be a lot of explaining of what happened. I just didn't feel like going through that process today. So I left to do my own thing, which was a real bad idea because I lived right around the corner where I sold drugs—very convenient; I could walk to work. Ha ha.

I was on the run now from the neighborhood thugs. If they caught me, I knew I was going to get a beatdown, but I chose to run. And that's the end of the story of whatever happened, I had to deal with it. I made my bed; now I have to lie in it. I was doing good ducking the people that were looking for me. Until one day a guy I knew from the neighborhood saw me. He told me that there was no problem with me coming back to work. They weren't mad that I left the block. I could sell drugs to work off what I owed them. I said that was great because

I was tired of ducking and hiding. Damn, he lied—they did want me to work off my debt, but they wanted to also beat me up just a little. I think the top man liked me, but what I did was disrespectful to him and his business. So he had to make an example out of me. So he whipped my ass in front of everyone. I was so embarrassed.

After he whipped my ass, he told me I better get the money I owed him. It was only $150—that wasn't a lot of money, but it was the principle of the act I committed. I was embarrassed by what just happened to me, but I was trapped in this lifestyle so I thought. I worked the debt off. I also got closer to the top man. He would give me extra money as a bonus. He would tell me that I was doing a great job because I would pick up my bundles earlier than the other workers. Why? I realized that I could sell two bundles in the morning around eight to ten. That was good for me, because I would feel sick in the morning. So I could get me a bag of P-Funk, so I could feel normal for the whole day.

The only thing about that I was moving deeper into that world of destruction. I started to lie and scheme even more than before. I used to be the guy that his word was his bond. If I gave you my word, you could count on it, but now my word wasn't shit. At that time in my life, I was noticing a change in myself. But I didn't want to stop it—it was exciting to me. I kind of liked the danger of the lifestyle. Believe me, I know selling drugs in your neighborhood isn't a good thing to do, but as I said before, I was on a self-destructive path to nowhere. I was working the corner, making my money to maintain my lifestyle of getting high on a daily basis. Until one day something came over me to run off with some bundles of crack.

I don't know why I was feeling like that—everything was going well. I was going upstairs to the apartment where all the drugs were kept. The other workers had to wait until the manager came downstairs with their bundles. He would come around twelve noon by that time of the day; I would have sold three to four bundles of crack already. So I did it again—I was on the run. I really had to duck and hide now. This was the second time I did this, but this time, the beatdown would be much worse. I would probably have to go to the hospital if they didn't kill me. I took three bundles: $450 worth of crack. Now that I think back on how little I thought my life was worth back then, to have someone hurt you or even kill you for $450 wasn't worth it, but back then I didn't think like I think now. In those days, I just wanted to get high and get me some pussy—that's what I did to have fun. So I found me a girl and went to the hotel. I had a great time that night until the morning came. It was reality time—I fucked up. I ran off with another package. This time I was dead—no questions asked. I had let that bad behavior take control of my life once again. Damn, where would I go? I tried to stay at a friend's house. He said no, I couldn't stay there. So I was kind of lost to where I would stay while I was on the run. Then it came to me: the homeless shelter on Wards Island. Yes, that would be the perfect place for me to hide out.

I found out about the shelter when I had robbed a friend's stash house and I needed somewhere to hide out. It was the perfect place because the people I knew would never stay in a shelter. You might say the shelter, I could never stay there. It wasn't that bad—it reminded me of Rikers Island. I had been there a couple of times for armed robberies. So I would act the same way I would if I was on the island. I was a warrior ready for whatever came my way.

The first time I went to jail, I was about thirteen years old. I was hanging out with some guys that liked to take money from people, so we started robbing prostitutes. We thought two wrongs don't make a right, meaning they were selling pussy and that's illegal. So robbing them would be all right—at least that's what we thought. Damn, how stupid we were to believe that. Until one day we had just robbed this trick for his money. We wouldn't rob the girls because they were hustling like we were. But that didn't work in our favor—it still was robbery. We got $250 from him. We were excited—it was a good lick. So we divided it up in three ways. Now, we had some money in our pockets, and it felt good. I was hungry, so I said let's get some fish and chips from the restaurant. They agreed. As we ordered our food, the cook told me that he had no more fish cooked—it would take twenty minutes to cook some more, but he did have chicken. I ordered some chicken and french fries.

He asked if I wanted to eat there or take it out. The guys were eating their food, so I got it to stay. We had finished eating. We were on the move again, looking for another trick to rob. When this white man said, "Come here," I started thinking, *have I robbed him before?*

Then he said, "Put your hands up—if you don't, I'll blow your fucking brains out." As I focused on what was happening, I saw five men with guns and badges. They were undercover detectives with the Robbery Task Force. We were arrested and taken to the precinct. They separated us to ask us questions. They treated me different; because I was a minor, they couldn't speak to me without my parents or guardian. My mother was out of town. So my aunt came to pick me up.

While I waited, I saw how the police worked their magic against us. How they would say whoever told the truth first would be the one that got the better deal. They said that I was going home, and the others were old enough to go to Rikers Island, where the killers and rapists were waiting for them. So they needed to tell their side of the story fast. I had two partners I did robberies with—JJ and Low. Now, JJ was the one that went for the bullshit the cops was telling him. We had already talked about what we would do when we got arrested. He must have forgotten what we talked about. I think he was scared of what might happen to him in jail.

So we asked JJ what he told the cops. He said he told them a little bit of what happened. The cops' magic was working—we haven't even been to court yet and we're turning on each other already. The cops are good at what they do. Low had already started saying that it's all about saving yourself. He said that self-preservation is the first law of nature, and he was going to follow the law to the letter. When my aunt came to pick me up, I felt alone. I didn't have any partners in crime like we talked about. We said we would die for each other—partners for life.

Thinking back on the incident, we were young, dumb, and full of come. We let our emotions and stupidity take control of our actions. That's always a bad move because we didn't think about what we were doing. We just did what we wanted. Now look where we're at: in jail. I was going home, but JJ and Low were going to Rikers Island with the big boys. The things I thought were fun were turning out to be my worst nightmare.

On my way home. I was thinking of how I was going to get out of this, but most importantly how was I going to tell my mother. Sometimes I think my mother was related to Clint Eastwood's character. Dirty Harry because she would say, "Go ahead—make my day." So I had to come up with a good story for her to understand why I was robbing people for their money. When I saw my mother, she asked me why I did it before I could answer her questions.

She slapped the shit out of me. Dirty Harry was on the set. She started asking me why I did it. To be honest, I was confused—did she want me to tell her what actually happened, or did she just want to beat me up? Eventually, she did calm down. I told her my story. She started to cry and say what she was going to do with me. I was such a problem. She didn't know what to do anymore—just let the court system have me. I was sad because I didn't want to hurt my mother's feelings. I wanted her to be happy and proud of me when she saw me, but that wasn't the case. When she saw me, I could see the hurt in her eyes for me. I tried to do better each and every day. It was like I was cursed with a bad spirit that would take control of me, making me do things I didn't want to do.

Now, that's some bullshit if I ever heard some. I didn't care about anyone's feelings back then. It was all about Sam the Man—now that's the truth being told. I realized now having an attitude like that was why I got in so much trouble. I thought I knew it all, and no one could tell me anything. I learned the hard way; that's why I'm writing these stories of mine down. To maybe help someone that might be going down the same path of danger. I feel if I can help one person change their path in life, then I have done my job as a good citizen in America. That's what I'm working toward now in my life, creating good karma in my community by helping others as much as I can.

I had to go to family court for the robbery case I had against me. I got one-year probation for my act in the robbery. I lost the friendships I had with JJ and Low. They really went through the court system because they were seventeen and nineteen years old. They didn't like that I didn't spend any time on Rikers Island. They were so mad that they made up stories that my mother and I were the ringleaders of the robbery team. They said she would tell them what areas to hit. It had gotten real crazy; I learned those guys weren't my friends. Even today I'm very cautious about how I chose my friends. I think the distrust from those guys messed me up bad. I mean it really damaged my trust for other people. That distrust in others led me to become a loner, not having a lot of close friends, just associates.

This is good, in a way, because you have different people to hang out with. But you don't have a solid friendship—that's what I've always wanted and needed. From not having solid friendships, I went from friendship to friendship, trying to find the right match. Now, that has led me into some one-sided relationships that would get me into trouble. Sometimes I would end up in jail, like the time I met these guys. They were a real stickup crew. They woke up in the morning, talking about what their next job would be. I wanted to be down with them. So the next robbery, I would be in the mix with them. They planned to stick up a Chinese restaurant. I was the lookout. I was supposed to stand in a doorway next to the restaurant to make sure no one followed them when they came out of the restaurant. But I was drunk from drinking beer, so I decided to stand at a bus stop right in front of the restaurant. I had a shotgun with me that was wrapped up in a coat. While standing at the bus stop, I dropped the coat, and this lady saw the shotgun. She started screaming, "He has a gun!" A man tried to take the shotgun. So I picked it up and ran, leaving the guys behind unprotected because the man was chasing me. So I threw the gun because it was making me run slower. I thought to myself I would duck him, then come back later for the gun.

The next thing I knew there were two police cars in front of me. The cops had their weapons drawn, telling me to put my hands up and that I was under arrest. He also asked me where my crew was. I said, "Officer, I just got off the bus. I was coming from my girlfriend's house." While I was thinking of the lie I was about to tell, I'm controlling my breathing because I had been running.

Then the man that had been chasing me said, "That's him and here is the shotgun."

I said, "Officer, that's not my gun."

He looked at me and said, "Yea right—it's yours now." I was on my way to Rikers Island again for armed robbery. I wasn't a minor this time, so my mother or guardian couldn't come to pick me up like before. This time I was going to the Big House.

I started preparing myself for the journey I was about to partake in. I went to court. The judge sent me to the island for seven days. The day I came back to court, they couldn't find the shotgun, so the judge released me to go home. I was so happy the judge let me go home. I was living with Ms. Jones at the time. She was the mother of one of my school friends. I started staying with them right after my mother was murdered. I was around seventeen or eighteen years old. I had moved out of my mom's for a couple of years. She lived in Manhattan in Wagner Projects. I lived in the Bronx with a woman named Tina. She was twenty-five years old and had a little girl. All I did when I stayed with her: I would take care of her daughter and have sex with her. She was one of my earlier teachers of the sex game: how to make a woman say, *damn, that's my spot.*

I was staying with Tina for about a year when my mother told me she was having trouble with her boyfriend, Joe. She said he threatened to kill her. I thought I knew Joe because we use to talk about manly things. So I told her that he was just talking because he was mad at her. I told her not to worry because I would stop by her house later. I never did go back to her house. I started getting high, but that night I couldn't get high. I drank beers and sniffed P-Funk. I couldn't get high—I just got angry at everyone, especially Tina. I even told her to go sleep in her daughter's room.

We eventually made up by having sex. So when Tom came to tell me my mother was dead, I was naked. He told me he had something to tell me. He wanted me to go into the other room with him, but I was naked and I didn't feel like getting up. Plus, I thought it was about some girls we were fucking. So I said, "You can tell me in front of Tina."

He said, "Your mother has been murdered."

I said, "Man, don't play like that—if you want to tell me something, don't use her like that." I looked him straight in his eyes. I saw that he was telling the truth. I saw the hurt in his eyes. Tina said get dressed and go see what happened. I got dressed and went over the adjoining roof to my father's apartment. My father and I didn't have a good relationship. I'll tell you about that later. When I knocked on his door and he found out it was me, he asked me what I wanted. I told him I think my mother has been murdered. Then he opened the door for me. He let me call my mother's house; a police officer answered the phone. Now, it was Sunday morning—no cop was supposed to answer my mother's phone. The officer told me that my mother's house was a crime scene and that I needed to go to the hospital because there was a little girl that was hurt also. The little girl was Joan; she was my mother's boyfriend's daughter. When I got to the hospital, I was a little nervous to see what happened to Joan. She had a black eye, it looked like someone had repeatedly beat her in the eye.

I mean it was very big and bruised. The police officer at the hospital told me that she also was raped. I later found out that her hymen was never broken. So was she really raped? It was so many stories about this murder. I didn't want to know what really happened that night. I left the hospital to go to my mom's house. The police was still in the neighborhood asking questions. A guy I knew came up to me and said, "Before you go upstairs to your mother's house, let's smoke this joint of weed I have." I smoked the joint, but it didn't make me feel any more relaxed than I was before I smoked the joint. I was still nervous about what I was about to see.

The police officer opened the door to the apartment. They were everywhere in that two bedroom apartment. I asked where she was at. A cop said, "In the back bedroom, but I don't think you need to see her like that." I said I wanted to see her, so he let me see her. She was lying there with her throat cut and multiple stab wounds in her body. When I saw her lying there, I felt numb for a few seconds. Then reality brought me back to earth. I don't remember crying the day of her death. I think I was in shock—to this day I don't remember some of the things that happened that day. I believe my mind pushed those moments of that day way back into a secret chamber and threw the key away. Now, this is why I self-medicated with drugs and alcohol for so many years.

I probably should have seen a counselor for what I had went through. I had lost my mother, and the police left me in the apartment alone with my mom's body until the coroner came. Now, that was a very uncomfortable time I had to deal with because it took them forever to pick up the body. I had time for all kinds of thoughts that came across my mind. I thought if I had came back like I said I would, maybe she would still be alive, or I might be dead too. How would I find the person that committed this crime and changed my life forever and forever? I didn't have a clue to how I was going to handle my life. I just lived my life one day at a time.

After the funeral, everything calmed down. I realized I was alone because my father had remarried. He had a daughter by his new wife, so he had to take care of his family. He didn't have time for me, so I went to the streets even more. I started hanging out with stickup crews—these guys were the real thing. They would train throughout the day by doing push-ups, jumping rope, doing pull-ups and sparring with each other because at night, they would walk up to the biggest dudes and take their money by force if they had to. I remember one day they approached this guy. They asked him for his money; he said get the fuck out of my face, so two of them started punching him in his face. While they were hitting him, they would say things like why you hit my sister, or why you rob my mother?

The guy would say I don't know who you're talking about. And they were right—it was just a distraction to make people mind their business. It worked like a charm. I would hear people saying, he shouldn't have messed with their family. Everything was going fine with the crew. I was making money doing robberies with them, but there was a young lady that I had dated before I joined the crew. Now, she was dating one of the guys in the crew. But this guy went to jail a lot, so when he was locked up, I would take care of his girl. If you know what I mean. we would have sex—I mean real passionate sex. Every time he went to jail, she would knock on my door. I was a gentleman—I couldn't leave a lady in need of attention stranded. Until one day I walked her to his mother's house. He found out about it, and I became an enemy of the crew instantly. One night I was at a party, I saw a guy from the crew with a nice ring on his finger.

I said, "That's a real nice ring you have on your finger."

He saw that I was wearing a leather jacket. So he said, "I like your jacket and you like my ring, so let's fight—the winner gets everything."

I said, "That's all right." I wasn't interested in fighting for those things. I started to leave, but he attacked me in the lobby of the building. I turned and hit him with an umbrella I had. We wound up on the floor with him on top of me. I took a couple of punches to the face, but I blocked most of them. He saw that I was blocking most of his punches.

I heard him yell to someone in the crowd, "Give me a knife so I can cut this motherfucker." That's when I looked up—I saw the front door of the building. At that moment, I pushed him off of me and ran for my life. I ran for a couple of blocks in the rain. It was raining like cats and dogs that night. I was soak and wet down to my underwear. I stopped to smoke a cigarette. I thought I had gotten away from the fight. When this guy grabbed me from behind, I tried to fight him off, but he won. I realized it was one of the guys from the crew that I was cool with. He told me that "you have to go back and fight because if you didn't, the crew would say you're a punk and a faggot. I don't think you want that title put on your name."

So I went back to fight. Now I was fighting a totally different person than before. I fought him in the rain for about ten minutes. The crowd was only five people now—the excitement was gone. It was about building a reputation with the crew for the guys that wanted to fight me because after fighting for ten minutes in the rain, he said, "Let's go to the park to finish the fight."

I told him, "Let's act like we went to the park, but I go home. You go back to the crew and tell them you beat the shit out of me." He said okay because he really didn't want to fight anyway. It was just to fit in with the crew, so I went home. When I woke up that day, my face was swollen. I had a black eye, and my body was sore as hell, hurting all over from head to toe.

I later found out that Tina's boyfriend was friends with the stickup crew, and he asked them to beat my ass to teach me a lesson for messing with his woman. I later found out he wasn't pleased with the beatdown they gave me. And it wasn't over with him—he wanted them to really hurt me bad. I mean put me in the hospital with some broken bones. Honestly, the sex was good, but not that good to go into the hospital for, or get a broken bone for.

I got me a ticket to go south. Augusta, Georgia, was my destination. I felt I needed to get away from this crazy lifestyle. It wasn't the lifestyle— it was me because when I got to Augusta, I experienced some of the same things I did in New York City. The drugs, drinking, fighting, and stealing—I did it all in Augusta. I realized that I had problems, but you have to want to change to get results. I know back then I wasn't ready to change. Honestly, I didn't want to change who I was. I liked the drama that came with the things I did. I thought that's how my life was supposed to be. I looked at my family; they were all drinkers and drug addicts. I also had some aunts and uncles that would beat the shit out of you if you pissed them off. So looking at my family's history, I was following the right path. But I always felt like something wasn't right. Like a part of me wasn't being fulfilled. So I really struggled with being the true me for many years.

I realized that's why I always included getting high in my everyday activities. I know I was hiding from myself. I realized that I wasted so many years of my life. I sometimes think if I would have gone the straight path for my life. I mean no drugs, no stealing, or going to jail—how much more would I have been a productive individual? People tell me that I have lived the life that I was supposed to live. If I hadn't went through some of the things I went through, I wouldn't be able to help the people I'm helping by writing this book. So the things I went through were just for me to help people with some of the same things I went through myself. Now, does that make my experiences less harmful to me? I mean, do I welcome what happens to me in my life? No, and I wouldn't want to go through it again. However, I do understand I can help other people by what I've been through in my life. It's kind of like Jesus Christ—he gave his life to save the people of the world for them to have a better life. I'm not saying I'm Jesus Christ. I'm just using an example to explain what I'm talking about.

I lived in Augusta, Georgia, for three years. I had a good job working for the Medical College of Georgia as a custodian in housekeeping. That was a pretty good job with benefits, but I wasn't ready for the stability. I still was hurt and confused from the loss of my mother. So I drank to ease the pain. I drank so much, I became an alcoholic.

I thought the drinking would help with the things I was going through, like missing my mother or having her to help me through my growing years to become a man. I did that alone with the help of a bottle of gin. I would get drunk and go to the cemetery to talk to her grave. I would sit there, talking and sometimes crying, telling her my problems and how much I missed her. I don't know if she heard me, but it made me feel better. I would do that at least once a week. I used that to heal myself from the pain, but at the time I didn't know that would help me. I was just going where I felt comfortable, and that was the place.

Along with the drinking came other problems like going to jail for public intoxication almost every weekend. It got so bad that a couple of times the police officers brought me to my grandmother's house instead of arresting me. I feel like that was a blessing, but I needed help and no one helped me. So I continued that cycle for the time I stayed in Augusta.

I ran into some rough characters in Augusta. I met this guy Tim. We became friends. We started breaking into businesses. One night, we were trying to break into these trailers. When the police showed up, we started running through this field. He went one way, and I went the other way. All I heard was running and someone falling than getting back up to run some more. I fell once—that was enough for me. I fell into a hole and I stayed there until I thought the police had left.

I hid in that hole for about an hour. When I came out, the police weren't around, but back then I didn't trust anyone—not even the police. So I needed a distraction for the police, if they were still in the area. I saw a young lady walking alone, so I walked up to her and started talking to her. She looked at me like I was crazy, but it worked out. I didn't get arrested that night. The next day I saw Tim. We laughed about what happen the night before. However, we never did that again. Our friendship slowly ended.

Then I met Bob—he was a pretty cool dude. We became friends instantly because we were both lost boys in this bad world. We would hang out, playing pool, drinking liquor, and stealing. He liked to steal, so we would go to the mall to steal record albums. We would always get the latest artist's albums so they could go fast. I never stole any of the albums. I was the lookout man. I never had the nerve to steal like that. You had to be very cool not to draw attention to yourself. Bob had it—he was as cool as a cucumber. He would walk in and go right to the new releases, get what he wanted, then walked right out. He was on a mission that he had to complete. The funny thing about it we never got caught, but when he went by himself, he got arrested. After that I never went back to the mall to steal anymore. After his arrest we still hung out, but I stopped going with him to steal. I found a job at the Medical College of Georgia as a custodian.

Even though I was working, I still was a troubled guy. Like the time I found my grandfather's German Luger—it shot twenty-two longs and held ten bullets in the clip. I would always keep one in the chamber because you have to be ready at all times. Thank God I never had to be that ready and use it on someone. But let me tell you that guns and alcohol don't mix. I remember coming out of the club one night. People were hanging out in front and standing by their cars because the club just closed. I was so drunk—the liquor told me to shoot in the air. I shot the gun in the air. Everyone started running like roaches for cover. I thought that was so funny at that time. Today I think that was very immature. I could have hurt someone, or I could have been arrested. I wasn't—that's why I think I continued to do stupid things that could have sent me to jail for a while. The one thing that would have helped me so much would have been the support of my family. I needed them to help me through my hard times, but they weren't there for me. I don't think they knew how to help me; all I needed was their love—that's all. Because I felt alone. I had just lost my mother. Now that was a lot to handle all by myself. I feel I had no choice—it was me and the liquor on a daily basis, fighting whatever came my way. I did hang out with my family sometimes at the club. We would laugh and drink together, but we never talked about what was happening with me in my life.

The reason I feel like this is because my mother had six sisters and four brothers. I should have had more family support. That's why I decided to leave New York City. When I was having so much trouble in NYC, I thought Augusta would be better because I had a big family there. That's why I went there. I also knew my mother had six sisters. I thought one of them would step up to be a second mother to me, but that didn't happen. I did get some support, but not the support I needed. It was kind of weird though. I was hanging out with one of my uncles, going to the club, playing pool, and drinking liquor. I thought we were building a strong family relationship when we got into two fights—one over my grandfather's gun, and the other over a female. After the two fights, I felt hurt and betrayed that he would attack me like a stranger. I slowly moved away from the family house my grandmother lived in. I got me a room of my own. I would see my family. I would say hello to them, but I kind of kept my distance from them. I felt it was safer to do it like that. I realized that they could hurt me because I was an emotional wreck. I just needed love, but they didn't know how to give the love that I needed. So I became a loner, handling my problems all by myself. Now, that strategy was good—it kept me safe. But I would never trust anyone else with my feelings. I also drank a lot of liquor at that point in my life.

I drank so much I would black out and not remember what happen the day before which wasn't good at all. One of my biggest fears was me doing something and getting arrested for it, but not knowing what I've done. Having someone else telling me what I had done—now that's some scary shit to go to jail for something you know nothing about. I would say I was the walking dead back then. I would black out from drinking too much alcohol. I blacked out every weekend because that's when I drank the most liquor. I couldn't get the drugs like when I was in NYC. The quality wasn't very good. They put smaller amounts in the packages to sell to you. That's why I drank so much liquor: it helped me to medicate myself through the pain. However, the alcohol got me in more trouble than the drugs. I was arrested for public intoxication almost every weekend.

Looking back on my life, I wonder how I made it through those years of my life. It was all God in heaven guiding me through this process. One day I saw a picture on the wall. The name of the picture was Foot Steps in the Sand. When I saw that picture, the words on the picture said, *I was carrying you all the time*. And there was only one set of footprints in the picture. I knew I was blessed. That's why I went through the things I went through to help people like me. I know God was watching over me. I went to a church revival because someone invited me.

I was sitting there, watching the spiritual show. They sang songs about the Child of God. How he gave his life so we could live. The show was very good because I started to feel the spirit of the Lord come over me. I was trying to hold back my emotions, but the spirit came over me to the point that I couldn't control myself. I started to cry. I tried not to cry, but I couldn't stop crying. That's when I knew I was blessed to bless others, but I continued to run. I wasn't ready for the calling that was on my life. To take on a calling from God is no joke. I was raised by a woman that taught me not to play with God's word. She also taught me that when you're ready, you'll know. I wasn't rushing my calling to help people because I wanted to do it right when I was ready. I knew I would not be perfect when I accepted the calling, but I wanted to do it to the best of my abilities, so I could be a role model to the ones I come in contact with.

I really missed New York City. At first, I missed it when I saw a music video or a TV commercial with scenes from NYC. I started thinking about New York City every day. I even started dreaming about it—going back home was heavy on my mind. So I called my dad to see if I could come home. It had been a couple of years since he had seen me or talked to me. He trusted that I had changed for the better—at least that's what I told him. I was excited that he said I could come home because Augusta, Georgia, and I never really got along anyway. I started telling people that I was going back home to NYC. Some people were happy for me, and others weren't happy. They were just jealous that I was moving on to a new chapter in my life and they were staying in Augusta. The only thing that was different between us was they were afraid to take a chance, to take a risk in their lives, and I wasn't afraid. I was always very curious about things. That's why I started using drugs. I was curious about how they made you feel.

I think I should have kept that one locked away and thrown the key away in the ocean, but I didn't—I was back on the streets of NYC. My dad lived in the Bronx—not much different than Manhattan. I was a New Yorker; I could fit into anywhere with no problem. Plus I lived with him before I went down south. I was just excited to be back in New York City. I started seeing some of the old people from the neighborhood like Tina. She stopped by, and I took care of her milk and cookies (we had sex). The relationship wasn't the same. It was different; she was really getting high. I mean she was deep in the drug game. I never really was into street girls. I liked my woman to be a homebody that's street-smart but also book-smart so she could handle herself in both arenas. I always felt the man's job was to make his money any way he can, but his woman would take care of the children and the household.

Now, if both of y'all are running the streets, who's taking care of the children and your home? No one. And if you get locked up, who's going to help you through the process until you get out of jail? Also if you have children, the mother lays the foundation for their lives. What kind of person would they become if their mother and father are in jail?

Now that I was back in the Big Apple, I had to find an income. I needed a job. My father was a hardworking man that believed a man must work if he wants to eat. So if I wanted to continue staying with him, I needed to find a job fast, but my mind wasn't on working a job. I wanted to hustle in the streets to sell cocaine or heroin. I could make it happen because I had a plan. I was getting a check from my job in Augusta for sick and vacation time. The check was for $2,000. Now that would be a good start for hustling. I brought a thousand dollars' worth of cocaine. I had a gun (25 automatic) and two guys to help me sell the cocaine. I also had about a thousand dollars for spending money. Now, that was the perfect drug dealer start-up kit. But the one thing I didn't have was the cold ruthless heart needed to be successful in the drug world. I also trusted the two guys in my crew too much. I later found out they were using the cocaine themselves instead of trying to sell it at the bar. I also gave a friend of mine a package of cocaine. He was a cokehead too. He fucked up that package too.

Now this is where the cold ruthless motherfucker was supposed to show up, but he didn't because that wasn't who I was. So I lost everything I did. Like everyone else, I got high on my own supply. I sold the gun for some coke because the whole thing was a real disaster. I knew then I was going to be a user of drugs. I'm not saying I didn't sell drugs. I did, but I was a worker, not the boss. So I still could get my own drugs on a daily basis that would help me deal with the pain I experience every day. That worked for a while, but I had to deal with getting arrested for selling drugs almost every day.

Now, that's a very stressful thing to deal with. I wouldn't only use drugs for the pain. I would use them to deal with the fear of being arrested. When I was high, I had no fear—I was fearless. That's how you had to be if you wanted to make some money selling drugs. I didn't make a lot of money because I was a dope fiend. I call myself that because it was about the high for me, not the money. I remember times I would be selling crack from ten in the morning to twelve o'clock at night. And I would have no money to show for the work I had done for all those hours. I would have enough money for a dollar can of mackerel for my dinner. I did make money for selling crack cocaine. I made $15 off every bundle I sold. I sold about five to ten bundles a day, but sometimes the corner would get very busy and I would sell more. So there was no reason I should have been eating a dollar can of processed fish.

Like I said, I was a dope fiend. I can't say I was proud of being that because when I was sober, I didn't like the person I saw in the mirror. I would see I needed a haircut and some new clothes. I was a shy person. I also was afraid to approach women. The drugs and alcohol gave me the confidence I needed. When I looked in the mirror, the image I saw was fine. I didn't need a haircut; my clothes were all right. And I was a ladies' man with many female friends.

I thought for many years, I needed drugs and alcohol to help me be the person that I was. I know that's not true. I believe I learned that behavior from the environment I was raised in—everyone I was around was in that lifestyle. So I just followed the crowd because I thought that was what I was supposed to do. The adults in my life at that time drank alcohol, and the teenagers that I hung out with used drugs, so I did what I was around. I know now if you want to be successful in life, you have to be different from the crowd. Meaning you have to sacrifice some things in your life to be successful like not cutting classes in school, doing your homework, and saying no to drugs and alcohol. Also having a plan, following it, and having someone to hold you accountable for your actions are an important key to your success. If you look at any successful person most likely they had a coach, mentor, big brother, or parent that helped them through the process of becoming successful.

I believe if you change your environment, you can change your destiny. By changing your destiny, you can change the future of your children. By changing the destiny of your children, you can change the future of your children's children. This can be done by sacrificing some of your time toward something that's positive. It can help you become successful, but it can also determine your future and your family's future. I believe everyone wants to be successful and have the finer things in life. However, everyone isn't willing to do the sacrificing that's needed to gain those things. Just think: if you wanted something bad enough, you would do anything to get it, like breathing air—you need it to live. Without it, you die.

I remember the first time I shot heroin in my arm. It was a summer day. Everyone was sitting on the stoop in front of the building. I was sitting on the stoop with nothing to do. Just watching people that is something I like doing. People's behaviors are interesting—you can learn so much if you watch them.

All of a sudden, I heard someone call my name. It was Paul. He said to come upstairs to his apartment. I knew him from the neighborhood. We would talk sometimes when he wasn't busy going somewhere. I always thought he was a cool guy who had it all together. When I got upstairs to his apartment, I saw a totally different Paul. He was sweating and shaking. I got scared when I saw him. I asked him if he was all right—did he want me to call for an ambulance to take him to the hospital? He said he was fine. He just needed me to make a run for him. Like a knucklehead, I went to buy four bags of dope for him. He told me to only get Sexy Lady because that was the best shit out there. He said he needed the good shit to feel normal again.

When I came back, he was ready for his medicine. He had everything set up. I didn't know that this would be my first time shooting heroin. He did his thing. Now he was the Paul I would talk to when he wasn't busy going somewhere. That's the guy I liked. He said, "I saved you a taste—do you want it?"

I said, "Hell yea" because I thought he was so cool. He wrapped my arm up to get a vein.

He looked me right in my eyes and said, "Are you sure you want this?"

I said yes. That was one of the biggest mistakes I made in my life. However, the first time I felt like I was floating on air without a care in the world. My body got all warm, and I felt so relaxed. I was Mr. Cool. I loved it. I didn't know that after making that decision, I would become a slave to shooting heroin for years. I also became Paul's runner. He would call me to cop or pick up his medicine, as he would say. I did that for a while until he got busted for armed robbery. I think he was trying to rob a store on the Avenue.

After his arrest I was alone. I had a habit that I had to take care of on a daily basis. That monkey would ride my back until I got a bag of dope. Some days it was easy, but there were days that were hard as hell to make it through. I don't know how I did it, but I made it through that time of my life—thank God. I thank God for helping me through that journey of my life. I also think I was the kind of dope fiend that got high off of everything. So whoever I was with, I did what they did. If they took pills, drank alcohol or beer, snorted or shot cocaine or heroin—whatever they did, I did.

So when I got sick from not getting my bag of dope, I used other things to help me feel normal. I also had all kinds of friends that I would learn different things from. I think that's what helped me. It also hurt me too because I trusted people too much. People are funny when you first meet them. They're so nice—they give you their time and attention. That's just a trap to get you to let your guards down. Then the real person comes out to take control of the relationship you thought you had. You might say that's not true, but I'm speaking from my own experiences. I can't talk about yours, but if you have people around you that empower you, then you're where you need to be. You should embrace your environment and use it to accomplish your goals to have a successful lifestyle.

I have done that—I used to hold drugs and use drugs to get high with different people. I used to stand on the corner, steering people to buy drugs from me. I took those same skills I learned. I turned those skills into becoming a people's person and a great networker. I went to a lot of networking events in the city trying to meet people to help me change my environment and to also help me build my consulting business. I realized that people always need help, so just like I helped people buy drugs, I now help business owners build their businesses with whatever they need. If they need funding for their project, I would find an investor for a percentage of the deal. I also helped them find attorneys, real estate agents, and contractors. To be honest, I would find them whatever they needed to finish their project. Sometimes I didn't make any money, but it is not always about making money. Building a strong business relationship can be worth millions of dollars. Then you'll start making money from the referrals that came from the relationships you built with them.

I think it's who you know that is the key to success because if you don't know something, you can learn how to do things you don't know how to do. So develop real relationships because you never know how far they can go. It's who you know that's the key to success.

The power of a relationship saved my life one day. I had done a robbery or two with these guys. When I got arrested, the police took a shotgun from me that one of the guys let me hold to do the robbery. It was about six of them, so I would run into one of them all the time. They would ask for money because I lost the shotgun. I felt that I got arrested; the cops took the weapon that was a part of doing a crime like armed robbery. They felt I owed them some money for the shotgun. I had a couple of encounters with those guys. The first time we had a fight in the pool hall, I hit the leader with a pool stick. After that, they always approached me with a gun, telling me that they didn't want to shoot me—they just wanted money for the shotgun.

One day I was walking with Lee. She was a very close friend of mine. She taught me how a man and a woman could be friends without having sex. Before I met her, I was totally against women being my friend. If I wasn't having sex with them, then I didn't need them as my friend. But with her, we were more than friends—we were partners. She was a better friend than any male friend I ever had. We were walking down Second Avenue to get a bag of P-Funk. When these two guys came up to me, they said, "You're Earl, right?" I just stared at them because I knew they were looking for trouble. They told me to take a walk with them. I still was trying to plan my escape. So I quietly thought about my plan of escape.

Then all of a sudden Lee started yelling, "Hell no, he isn't walking with you guys nowhere. If you're going to shoot him shoot him right now because he isn't going anywhere with you guys!" They told me to make her shut up and stop yelling. She started yelling louder and saying, "If you're so bad shoot him right here show us how bad you guys really are!"

They said to each other, "Let's get the fuck out of here." They looked at me and said, "It's not over we'll see you again soon so watch your back." Then they walked away. I was shocked and happy at the same time because what Lee had done had really worked. From the relationship we had as friends, she put her life on the line for me. So building a strong relationship with people does pay off in the long run. The example I gave was kind of extreme, but if I didn't have a strong relationship with Lee, I might not be here to tell you this story. I have another story of how a relationship saved my life. I was hanging out with Rose; she was another close friend of mine. Big Al stopped by. He had some cocaine he wanted to shoot. So I let him use the back bedroom to do his thing. He left me a taste of cocaine in the cooker for letting him use the room to shoot his cocaine. If I would have said no, it would have cost him a lot more than a little bit of coke in his cooker. So he was thankful for my help, and I was happy for the coke he gave me. I drew the coke up in a needle. Then I tied up my arm to make it easier for my veins to pop up. I saw a good vein to use. I took the needle and stuck it in my vein. I then shot the coke into my body. I started to feel a rush come over my body.

Now that's where the trouble starts because I liked the rush that comes over my body. So I booted the blood in my vein (drawing the blood back and forward in the needle) to keep getting the rush. I always did that when I shot coke, but this time the coke was real good. It was so good I passed out. I overdosed on the cocaine. I was out cold. Rose saw that I was out and not moving. She said she called me a couple of times, but I didn't respond. She then slapped me in the face. I still didn't answer her. She tried to get help from someone in the house, but Big Al had left. She was there all by herself. She told me that she didn't want me to die. So she thought about her brother—he had overdosed on some coke before, and they put him in the tub and turned the shower on, letting the cold water run over him. The cold shower worked for her brother, and it might work for me. She picked me up and dragged me to the bathroom. Then she dropped me in the tub. She turned the cold shower on me, and yes, it did work. I woke up quick and fast. I was thankful she cared enough not to let me die, but when she dropped me in the tub, I hurt my hip real bad to the point that I couldn't walk. I had to use a cane to help me walk around. I was hurt so bad I couldn't go to work or hustle. I lost a lot of weight— people thought I had AIDS. I didn't have the virus thank God. I just wasn't eating enough food to keep the weight on me. I stayed in the house for about a month, so my hip could heal. I did get high, but only when someone gave me something to get high on.

There have also been times when relationships haven't been good for me. I've had relationships that were one-sided. I would give my time and work hard to be a good friend. It never worked out because the person that I was friends with was a selfish person. It was always their way if it wasn't their way, then I would have problems. Like when I had money and they wanted to get high, they would ask me for some money. If I said no, they would put me out of the house. That happened a couple of times. One time it was snowing. He got mad because I didn't want to get high or give him money to get high.

There were times that I was trying to stop using drugs, and that was one of those times, but he didn't understand that I wanted to stop using drugs. Like I said, he was a very selfish person. If he wasn't in control of what was happening he would get mad. But when he had money, he wouldn't share with me. If he did it wasn't like how I shared with him. I would buy him a whole bag of P-Funk for himself. He would give me some of a bag he brought and watch how much I took out of the bag. I would also hang out with him the whole day until all my money was gone. He would leave me in the house. He would say he would be right back, but he wouldn't come back for hours. When he came back, he was high as hell with no money. He would go into his bedroom and close the door. Sometimes he would bring me a half of a bag of P-Funk to try and make me feel better. I would accept the drugs because I was a drug addict.

But I didn't like the feeling I would get when he did that. One day, a friend of mine saw how I was feeling. He said, "I see you don't like how you're feeling. The only way to stop that feeling is to change what you do when you get your money. If he doesn't share all his money with you, then maybe you should limit how much you share with him and see how much he likes it." He didn't like it, but I started to take control over what I did. To start taking control over my life felt good because there were times I would do things for him that I really didn't want to do. I was afraid that if I didn't do what he asked me to do, he would put me out on the street, and I would be homeless. I stopped letting him have that kind of control over me. He was a real selfish guy. I was too trusting of him and others. I had to change who I was, not being so trusting of people.

Now let me explain: there's nothing wrong with trusting people. Believe me, if you have a group of people you trust, that's great. I'm just speaking about the people that I was around. They weren't trustworthy people. Sometimes I think about why they were like that—was it because they had a drug problem? Did the drugs control their behaviors, or were they just selfish people? I would like to believe it was the drugs, not them. I gave them the benefit of the doubt that their personality would have been different if the drugs weren't in their lives. I like to think like that about people because it helps me look at them in a better way.

Before they show their true personality, I had a teacher that told me everyone starts with a grade of 100 percent. Now what you do with your 100 percent is up to you. So that's how I look at folks now—I put them in groups of how trustworthy they are toward me and others. If they do something to lose some of their 100 percent, I don't hold it against them—I just store it in my memory bank. I try to understand the personality they have because I'll meet another person with the same personality and I'll know how to deal with that person, so that's my system and it works for me. I'm happy with it. The day my mother was murdered was the beginning of a cycle of nothing but trouble. I went to jail a number of times for different things, mostly armed robberies. I also stayed high or drunk most of the time. I think I was angry at myself. I was on a path to self-destruction. I can remember when I would wake up with robbing and stealing on my mind. I was on a mission to get someone's money. If I didn't have a weapon or knew somebody with one, I would go out and snatch a ladies' handbag. I could snatch handbags very well because I was a fast runner. I also had quick hands—that was what it took to snatch handbags from women because some of them would try to fight back. But if you did it quickly, you would catch them off guard before they knew what was going on. I had their bag and I was gone like the wind to get high.

I stopped snatching bags because I started feeling bad for the ladies. They would yell and scream when I took their bags. I also thought that I would get caught if I kept doing it. I was more of a quiet theft. I didn't want noise when I did a crime. It brought too much attention to the scene. One time I snatched this lady's bag. She yelled and screamed, "Help me—he snatched my pocketbook!" Then she just screamed. There were no words coming out of her mouth. Some guys saw what happened, and they started chasing me. So I threw the pocketbook at them, thinking that would stop them from chasing me. They caught the bag, but some of them continued to chase me. I started to get scared. I knew I couldn't let the two guys chasing me catch me. So I started running faster. I saw that they couldn't keep up with me. That's when I took advantage of the distance between us. I ducked into a building to hide from them. It worked—I hid in that building for about an hour. Then I came out slowly, making sure the guys had left.

After I started walking home, I felt safe, but you never know, so I was walking very fast. I found a piece of pipe that I carried with me. I felt unsafe, so I carried that piece of pipe all the way to my father's house. Now that was a scary night for me, but I didn't learn my lesson yet. I was on the train, not thinking about doing any crime at all.

When I saw this lady sitting on the train by the door, she was falling asleep. She would wake up when the train pulled into the station. I kept watching her and said to myself, "If she is asleep when my stop comes, I'm going to snatch her pocketbook." As the train got closer to my stop she went into a deeper sleep. When the train stopped on Longwood Ave., she was sleeping hard. I even think I heard her snoring—I mean she was out cold. When I saw she was knocked out, I kept my word to myself. I went to the door like I normally would to get off the train. While I was waiting for the train to stop, I looked up and down the train to see if anyone would be a threat to what I was planning to do. There was on one I felt threatened by on the train. So I snatched her bag once the doors opened up. When I snatched her bag, she woke up, but like I said before, I was quick when I made my move. I snatched her bag and jogged to the exit. I didn't run because that would bring attention to me. She did scream, but it was too late. The doors of the train closed, and the train was pulling out of the station. Once I was out of the subway, I started to walk. I needed to find a place where I could look into her bag because women have secret compartments in their pocketbooks that they hide money in, and I didn't want to miss any of the money she had. I felt I took the risk to commit the crime, so I must get all the money for my effort.

I found a place I could look through the bag real good. There were $80 in her purse, but I found a $100 bill in one of the secret compartments and $20 in another one. For a total of $200 now that's not bad for less than an hour's work. Now, I know you might say that's fuck up to take advantage of someone like that. I looked at myself as an opportunist. I was always looking for ways to make money, and that was one of the ways I chose. So it wasn't personal for me—it was just business. And when I got high, I didn't even think about what I did to get the money. That's why I had to stay high: because when I wasn't high, I felt guilty and paranoid about what I had done to people. So when I went to jail, I accepted it because it was a part of what I was doing.

However, I would have the mentality of a warrior when I got arrested. I started doing push-ups and sit-ups because I knew someone was going to challenge me. So I had to be ready because in jail, it's not like being on the streets. You can walk away from problems on the streets, but not in jail—you have to handle your problems as soon as they come your way. If you didn't, the word would go out that you're soft or a punk, and you don't want people thinking about you like that. I never had any problems when I went to jail. I would like to say that I never served any years in jail, just weeks and months. Well, it only takes one day to have problems in jail.

I think the reason I didn't have any problems when I went to jail was because I learned how to mind my own business. I didn't want to be a part of the in crowd or the crew. I learned that sometimes it's not you bringing the drama. It's someone else. You're just a part of the group. Being that you're a part of the group, you have to go down as a group. I never did think like that—that's why I always stayed by myself. Like I said, I became a warrior, preparing myself for the challenges that would come my way. I believe I was blessed to have gone through what I've went through. It has to be a blessing to be able to come out like I have—I don't look like an ex-drug addict. Some people have that permanent frown on their face. Now, don't get me wrong—there's nothing wrong with having a face like that. I've been around people that don't even know I used to use drugs until I told them. Sometimes that blows my mind, but then I would look at their faces or how they treated me. After I told them, it was different. I would never tell them I noticed how they changed toward me. Once they learn about my past life, I would sometimes feel hurt because I didn't think they would act like that toward me. As I get more years of sobriety (since 1989. I understand that's how people are when they haven't gone through the experiences themselves. Also if my past makes them act different toward me, then I don't need them as my friend because we all have a past.

There's something that everyone isn't proud of—we all have skeletons in our closets. So please don't be too quick to judge someone on what they've done. If they're the kind of people that are judgmental, then I didn't need those kinds of friends. They're just too hard to please—it's like you're always looking for their approval. Now that's a task I choose not to take. Why? Because with friends like that, you can't be yourself. You're always under the microscope, or walking on eggshells. That can be very stressful and make you go back to using drugs. So be true to yourself and pick your friends wisely. If you don't, you can mess up your life forever. You'll wound up in a group of people that are really not your friends.

In an environment like that, how can you become the best person you possibly can become? It would be very hard—you'll also have to think about staying sober. Now, which is more important to you: having friends that you think are on your side, or staying sober without any stress? I think I would choose staying sober over having friends. The longer you stay drug free, the more your life will change for the better. I'm a strong believer in the law of attraction. Whatever you put in the universe is what you get back. Example: if you speak positive words out of your mouth, then positive things will start to happen in your life. I tell this story to people that need to believe in themselves sometimes to help them stay motivated.

There were three frogs in a hole in the ground, trying to jump out of the hole. They started trying to jump out of the hole, but there were frogs standing around the hole. Telling the frogs that were trying to get out of the hole: it's too high, you can't do it, and you'll never make it— just stop trying. After a while, one of the frogs said, "You're right—it's too high for me to jump out," and he stopped jumping.

The other two kept jumping, but the bystanders continued to tell them it was too high to jump out. Eventually, the second frog stopped trying to jump out of the hole. He told the other frogs, "You guys are right—it's too high to jump out." However, the last frog kept jumping and jumping.

The other frogs continued to tell him, "It's too high for you to jump out. You're wasting your time." He continued to jump. Eventually he jumped out of the hole.

Do you know why he was able to complete his task? He was deaf. He couldn't hear the other frogs telling him he couldn't do it, so he kept trying until he did it. If you want to be successful, you'll have to be like the frog that got out of the hole. Not hearing the haters when they tell you that you can't do it. I strongly believe you set the path for your life—good or bad, you're in control. It's up to you which way you go. I believe people get stuck in a path and believe that's where they're supposed to be. All they have to do is change their mindset to another channel.

If they did, they would eventually see a change, but the problem with that is you have to believe in yourself and have the faith to see it to the end. If you stay focused on the changes you choose, your whole life will change. I know that change is hard sometimes, but it's worth it. I'm not saying a 360-degree change where you drop everything and start over again. If you can do that, that's great because everyone can't make a change like that, or even handle a change like that. So starting with the little things is sometimes the best way to start. There's no pressure on anyone. That's one of the key elements to a successful mindset. When you change the things you were doing, it doesn't bring you any stress at all. You want to stay away from things that bring you stress.

A couple of times, I tried to change my mindset by cleaning myself up to get a job. I've had some pretty decent jobs, but I wasn't ready for the responsibilities that came with having a job. One of my first jobs was working at the Waldorf Astoria Hotel as a busboy. I cleaned the tables after the customers finished eating their meals. It was a pretty good job. They had a union, a healthcare program, and paid sick time. All I had to do to get those benefits was to pass a physical. I couldn't pass the physical because I couldn't stay drug free for the exam. That's what I'm talking about—not being ready. I knew what the job had to offer.

I just couldn't control the mindset to say no to the drugs. I eventually lost the job. They saw the person I really was: a drug addict. They told me, being I didn't take the physical exam and almost starting a fire, that they had to let me go.

Oh yeah, I forgot to tell you about how I almost burned down a restaurant in the Waldorf Astoria. I was busing the area I was assigned to take care of. I cleaned up my station. I then when to the locker room to change my clothes. I punched my time card and walked to the train to go home. I was on the train when I realized that I might have left the coffee pot on the warmer. I was three stops from my house. I thought, *Do I go back to turn off the warmer, or do I go home?* I could have let someone else handle that. I thought to myself that it wasn't my responsibility—everything was safe and sound when I left that night.

However, I went back to make sure everything was good and the restaurant wasn't on fire. I worked a four-to-twelve midnight shift. At that time of the night, the trains ran much slower. That made me think of all kinds of things that could happen. Just think of the headlines on the local newspapers: "Busboy Burns down the Waldorf Astoria." I would definitely go to jail for starting the fire.

By the time I got back to the restaurant, I was nervous as hell, thinking the fire department would be there, putting the fire out. When I got off the train, I prepared myself for the worst, but when I got to the restaurant it was quiet. It was 3 a.m. in the morning. I went to my station where the warmer was. To my surprise, someone had turned the warmer off. I was happy that someone turned off the warmer, but just as I thought a guy came up to me and said, "You are so lucky. The coffee pot was glowing red when I turned it off."

He said, "If I hadn't turned off that pot, we would be looking at a different situation."

I said, "You're so right."

He said, "Just be more careful."

I said, "I will. Thank you and have a good night."

I left the restaurant to get back on the train. I remember giving thanks to God for giving me favor: the blessings of not letting the restaurant catch fire and burn down. After all that I went through that night, I slept so well. However, I became more aware of my responsibilities after that night. Now, I always double-check myself on things I'm not sure of. Example: I always check the stove to see if all the burners are off before I leave the house. I also double-check to see if the front door of my apartment is locked. It gets so bad sometimes. I get back on the elevator to check the door, or check the apartment to make sure everything is all right. I've done that after I have left the building, sometimes walking down the block. I would turn back around to check things out. I think the doubtful behavior I have comes from making the wrong choices and seeing the failures from the results.

That's something I continue to work on, but some things just stay with you. It doesn't matter how hard you try to change them—you still have to try until you're successful. I have some tools that have helped me change my life. These are tools I use on a daily basis.

- Stay away from negative people. People with negative attitudes are dangerous to your success in life.
- Treat people the way you want to be treated. If you treat people with love and happiness, that's what you get back. (The law of attraction is what you put out is what you get back).
- True love is unconditional. When you truly love someone, you accept them for who they are.
- Check people out for yourself. Never listen to others because the way someone else feels about someone may not be the way you feel about them.
- Create the person you want people to see in you. If you want people to see you as an honest person, then you do things that honest people do. Example: honest people don't lie and steal from other people.
- Be humble at all times. Don't let people take advantage of you, but pick your battles wisely.
- Real friends are hard to find. A real friend is with you when you're at your lowest, not just when things are going great for you.
- Having a team is better than doing it by yourself. Having a team to support you through your journeys in life is helpful.
- Always follow your gut feeling.: When you feel unsure about something, don't question that feeling—follow it. Example: if you feel doubtful about someone or something, wait before you make a decision.
- Think before you speak. What you say out of your mouth can get you in a whole lot of trouble, so please think before you speak. Words are very powerful. Try to always speak life into someone. I find that people like to be empowered, so use words to empower others.

These are some of the tools I use in my life on a daily basis. They help me through the ups and downs I deal with. I call them my toolbox of tools. You can use mine, or you can create your own. You definitely need a toolbox of tools to help you build a better you. It's like building a house—you need certain tools to build that house. However, you can build it without tools, but it would be much harder. Having a toolbox with the tools you need for success makes it much easier to finish the job. These are some of the tools you can put in your toolbox. These are some extra tools I have access to—you can never have enough tools.

1. Accept people for who they are. Don't look at what people can't do; work with who they are.
2. Respect your fellow persons. Respect goes a long way in life, so make respect a part of your lifestyle.
3. Stay focused on your goals. Do a little every day. Think of your goals as a rock that you need to break into little pieces. So if you clipped on the rock every day, eventually it will break into pieces, and your goals will be completed.
4. Don't force a friendship. Let it grow naturally. Find people that are like-minded like you to build a friendship.
5. Self-development is the key to success. You have to reinvent yourself. Find something or someone you want to become and become whatever that is.
6. Be honest with your feelings. If you're not honest with your feelings, you will be limiting your abilities to control your emotions.
7. Strive to be a good role model. If you're a role model to others, that will keep you focused on doing the right things.
8. Listening is the key to truly getting to know a person. When you listen, you'll learn a lot about that person because people like to talk about themselves.
9. Your appearance is very important. How you present yourself is very important because people remember what they see. So if you show them a thug, that's what they remember, and that's what you don't want them to see you as.
10. Have good eye contact. Looking at someone when they're talking to you shows that they have your full attention.

Even though I have these tools in my toolbox, I still have problems that are hard to handle sometimes. I deal with something called the shiny object syndrome. If it looks like it's going to be successful, then I wanted to be a part of it, even if I haven't finished what I was doing first. This isn't good because I leave a lot of things incomplete. I look like a person that's not stable. I hear people saying, "You have to focus on one thing at a time." I disagree with that because as a person, you have more than one title. You're a father or a mother, a husband or a wife, a brother or a sister, an employee or an employer. You do all of these titles some better than the others, but you do them. So when I'm told to do one thing at a time, I say we're all multitalented, doing more than one thing on a daily basis. However, I do agree that some people aren't multitalented.

They might not be able to handle too many titles, but we can handle at least three titles. If you have trouble being a multitasking, person then your life is somewhat limited because to really be productive in life, you have to do more than one thing. So if you aren't multitalented, you have to develop your skills, so you can become a person that's a resource to others. You need to develop your God-given talent: the talent you were born with. We all were born with a gift or talent from our heavenly father. You just have to find out what it is and develop it until you master that skill. If you do that, then you'll be in your zone. Your life would be so fulfilled because you're doing what you were created to do.

But sometimes it takes you years to find your purpose in life. If that happens, I believe you aren't wasting time. You're gaining the needed experience to do your purpose more effectively. I found out that my purpose was networking with others. I would stand on the corner and direct people to buy drugs from me. I was very good at that skill. So I turned that into meeting people in business and selling products to businesses. I went from standing on the corner directing people to doing things I wanted them to do. I learned you can make people do what you want them to do if you find out what they want. You can control them because people like to feel good.

So I realized that I had a talent of being a likeable person. I could approach someone and start a conversation without a problem. Now, I feel that's a skill because most people have a problem when it comes to meeting people. They're shy or afraid to approach people at events. If you're doing sales, being shy or afraid to speak to people wouldn't work well with you building your client's list. I'm just telling you I realized my gift, and I have developed it. I feel very confident when it comes to approaching people. So find your gift.

If you have trouble finding it, ask your friends or family. What do they see you do all the time? Take that information and develop that skill. Believe me, it works—try it.

I also found out that I was a talker. I like to talk. After learning that, I realized I'm always talking to someone about how they can change their life. How I'm able to do that is through all the experiences I've went through in my life. So that helps me to help others. I also realized that I have a kind spirit toward people. However, that has gotten me taken advantage of in the past. Now, I stay in control of how I help people with their problems.

I remember a friend of mine needed help paying their rent. In the past I would have given them the money to pay their rent, not even thinking about if I could afford to give them the money. I just thought a friend needed help, and I could help them. I would later find out that my so-called friends didn't feel the same way I did when it came to helping a friend. I always had to go to the bank to get some money or go without whatever I wanted. I could never depend on the people I thought were my friends. That would hurt me, but I would always give them the benefit of the doubt, that they would do it if they could. I wanted to believe that they were my friend.

After trusting them a couple more times, I realized they didn't have my best interest in mind. They were just using me for what I could give them. From those experiences, I only gave people what I want them to have. If they needed $100, I wouldn't give them the whole $100. I would see what I could afford to give them. Most of the times I would give them $20 or $30 to help them out. I felt good about doing that. I was helping them to get closer to the amount they wanted to get to. By doing it like that, I felt in control and I still was being helpful. After being in control of how I treated people for so many years, now I've learned how to say no to people and not feel bad about saying no. I feel that people need to go through their problems, so they can learn how to handle the ups and downs of their lives.

Going through things that are difficult would help you gain experience on how to deal with the issues in your life. It also makes you a better person to have an open heart. That can help you understand the things that are happening in the world. When you go through tough times in life, you understand things a little clearer. But I hope the tough times in your life didn't make you angry and closed to learning what you need to learn to become a successful person in society.

For example: when you see a baby chicken hatching from their egg, you could help them break the shell, but that baby chicken needs to go through the difficulties of breaking through the shell. If you helped them, you would be interfering with their growth process. If you watch the process, it looks like they're having trouble coming out of the shell. But be patient—the baby chicken will complete the process to become a new addition to the chicken coop.

Or look at the birthing of a horse coming out of its mother's womb. Once the baby horse hits the ground, they're on their own. They're struggling to stand up, but they fall down a couple of times, trying to get their footing so they can stand up stable. The people watching the birth of the baby horse could help them, but for that horse to become a strong horse, that process is needed, and the people watching the birth know that. So why don't we let others go through their process, but when it comes to human beings, we always interfere with their growth process. We want to help, and I think helping your fellow person is great. I believe there should be limits to how much you help someone out because you can interfere with their growth process. I believe you can live your life either negative or positive. I read a book by Robin Sharma, *The Leader Who Had No Title*. This book had some key strategies of how you can live your life. He talks about the ten human regrets. These will make you look at your life differently.

1. You reach your last day with the brilliant song that your life was meant to sing still silent within you.
2. You reach your last day without ever having experienced the natural power that inhabits you to do great work and achieve great things.
3. You reach your last day realizing that you never inspired anyone else by the example that you set.
4. You reach your last day full of pain at the realization that you never took any bold risk, and so you never received any bright rewards.

5. You reach your last day understanding that you missed the opportunity to catch a glimpse of mastery because you bought into the lie that you had to be resigned to mediocrity.

6. You reach your last day and feel heartbroken that you never learned the skill of transforming adversity into victory and lead into gold.

7. You reach your last day regretting that you forgot that work is about being radically helpful to others, rather than being helpful only to yourself.

8. You reach your last day with the awareness that you ended up living the life that society trained you to want versus leading the life you truly wanted to have.

9. You reach your last day and awaken to the fact that you never realized your absolute best, nor touched the special genius that you were built to become.

10. You reach your last day and discover you could have been a leader and left this world so much better than you found it. But you refused to accept that mission because you were just too scared. And so you failed and wasted a life.

Now, if you choose these key strategies, then you probably feel like you wasted your life. These are the regrets you can feel if you lead your life in a negative way.

Living your life negatively can make you depressed and very unproductive. To the point of you becoming a zombie (the walking dead)—you're just existing. To just exist is a waste of life. I feel you need to be positive about life. By being positive, that makes your life very productive. And Robin Sharma has some key strategies for a positive lifestyle. These are some of the things you need to think about.

1. You reach your end filled with happiness and fulfillment on realizing that you are all used up, having spent the fullness of your talents, the biggest of your resources, and best of your potential doing great work and leading a rare-air life.

2. You reach your end knowing that you played at a standard of concentrated excellence and held yourself to the most impeccable of standards in each thing that you did.

3. You reach your end in noisy celebration for having the boldness of spirit to have regularly confronted your largest fear and realized your vision.
4. You reach your end and recognize that you became a person who built people up versus one who tore people down.
5. You reach your end with the understanding that while your journey may haven't always been a smooth one, whenever you got knocked down, you instantly got back up; and at all times, never suffered from any loss of optimism.
6. You reach your end and bask in the staggering glory of your phenomenal achievements along with the rich value you have contributed to the lives of the people you were lucky to serve.
7. You reach your end and adore the strong, ethical, inspirational, and empathetic person you grew into.
8. You reach your end and realize that you were a genuine innovator who blazed new trails instead of following old roads.
9. You reach your end surrounded with teammates who call you a rock star, customers who say you're a hero, and loved ones who call you a legend.
10. You reach your end as a true leader without a title, knowing that the great deeds you did will endure long after your death and that your life stands as a model of possibility.

By following these human victories your life would be a lot more successful. On the last days of your life, you will feel like you have had a big impact on your life and that you have helped others accomplished their goals too, but the most important thing about being positive in your life is that you're doing what you were born to do. It helps your fellow man to become successful in life.

ABOUT THE AUTHOR

Samuel E. Underwood was born and raised in New York City. He was born in Sydenham Hospital on December 27, 1957. He grew up in Harlem and went to school there. He later moved to the Bronx, where he lived with his dad. Samuel celebrates thirty-two years being drug—and alcohol-free. That is why he decided to write this book—to help someone out there that might be going through some of the things he experienced. Through his experiences, he felt people could learn how to handle their issues a little better and not panic when life seems to overwhelm them. Just take a deep breath and use some of the tools in this book. In the beginning, Samuel said it was difficult for him. He stayed focused on his goal. Now he has multiple years sober from any substances that would distract him. Samuel knows staying focused is the key to his success. Samuel followed his plan now—he is speaking to people about their plan. Samuel is a strong believer in each one teaches one by doing this: you build communities that empower their people. So let's empower each other to a successful lifestyle.